He was my friend

Samuel Eric Turpin

7th January 1919–20th October 2014

by
David Howden Hume

for Samuel, Katie and Ciara

ISBN 978-1-909751-68-2

Printed by Nicholson & Bass Ltd, Belfast

Contents

Chapter 7

Chapter 8

Chapter 9

Chapter 10

Chapter 11

When I survey the wondrous cross
On which the Prince of glory died,
My richest gain I count but loss,
And pour contempt on all my pride.

Forbid it, Lord, that I should boast,
Save in the death of Christ my God!
All the vain things that charm me most,
I sacrifice them to His blood.

See from His head, His hands, His feet,
Sorrow and love flow mingled down!
Did e'er such love and sorrow meet,
Or thorns compose so rich a crown?

Were the whole realm of nature mine,
That were a present far too small;
Love so amazing, so divine,
Demands my soul, my life, my all.

Isaac Watts

Foreword

WHEN IN OCTOBER 2014 my dear Uncle Eric died aged ninety five, I was asked by his friend David Hume if I would like to write up some of his early days in a Foreword of a book he was planning to write of Eric's life. I was delighted to be included in this way, and the following is my attempt to do justice to the honour of opening such a venture!

Stradbally, Co. Laois, Ireland

My uncle Samuel Eric Turpin, known as Eric, was born on the 7th January 1919 and lived for the first ten years of his life in Co. Laois where his father and grandfather before him had had a large and prosperous shop in Stradbally.

The Turpin family were of Huguenot origin and this Calvinistic ethos was still evident in the Turpin household in which Eric was raised. Their faith was very important to the family and every Sunday was spent in worship. In the morning they attended the Anglican Church of Ireland and then for the boys, Sunday School. The morning's sermon was always a subject for discussion at Sunday lunch. In the evening the family attended the local Methodist service. Consideration and care for other people was very evident in their everyday life.

Eric's father, Samuel Turpin and his wife, Marie Mitchell, already had a son, Lex. When their second son Eric arrived two years later to the day; his father commented at the time "Rather strange, both children were born on the same date in January."

Eric's home was a happy one. His mother was young, in her early twenties, Samuel's second wife and much younger than her fifty two year old husband. Marie was vivacious and full of fun and gave a lot of attention to her two boys.

Sadly, this happy life was not to last. In 1921 Marie went to Dublin to have her third boy Claud, but never returned. Samuel wrote : "My dear wife Marie died at Denmark House on Friday 17th June at 10.15 a.m… ."

Samuel was devastated, and for his two young sons, Lex and Eric, life was never to be the same. In future years Eric said he could still remember that dreadful day when the news came, and also the day several weeks later when the new baby arrived home in Stradbally, without his mother.

Miss Smith, or Mick as she was known by all the family, came to look after the children and run the house. Ellen Kealy, the maid, was also a very important and loving person in Eric's life; he and Lex loved to visit her in her cottage at the back of the local Convent.

In April 1923 Lex and Eric started school at Stradbally National School. Their father wrote that "they were both greatly excited the day before and in the morning. I wonder how they will feel in the afternoon!"

As a child Eric was always the one in trouble so I am told!

Another childhood memory of Eric was as a very small child he went completely missing and was eventually found stuck in a rabbit burrow into which he had crawled. This, he told me, left him with a lifelong dislike of being confined in small places.

In 1930 Samuel decided to go to Dublin and the family moved to 22 Dartmouth Square, Leeson Park.

It is at this point that Eric takes over the telling of his story in his own words.

Kathleen Kennedy
Ballincar, Co. Sligo
February 2016

Chapter 1

**A talk by Eric Turpin to the Church of Ireland's Men's Society at
St. John's Church, Malone Road, Belfast in 2004**

Grandfather's shop

MY FATHER HAD a shop, which was built by my grandfather, in Stradbally, Co. Laois, and it was the only real shop in the village at that time. When he was 50, my father married my mother, who was 20 and they had three boys.

My father decided to sell the shop and enjoy life: however, sadly my mother died at the birth of my younger brother, so it was a very difficult time for my Dad. We were brought up by a lady who was a retired governess and housekeeper and we moved to Dublin when I was eleven.

My two brothers and I went to the same boarding school there, The King's Hospital. Then we all went to Trinity College – my younger brother Claude became a doctor and my older brother Lex entered the British Foreign Office, ending up as a British Ambassador. Since the age of twelve I had been fascinated by chemistry so I

Eric, standing, with his elder brother Lex and younger brother Claude, Stradbally 1921

Eric graduates from Trinity College, Dublin, 1940

graduated as an Organic chemist and did three very interesting years of research work.

Then suddenly and unexpectedly my life was disrupted by religion! I was brought up in the Anglican Church of Ireland and have remained loyal to them all my life, but it was in a Dublin Methodist church that I happened to meet up with a group of Trinity students who presented me with the revolutionary thought:

"God has a plan for the world and everyone has a part to play and if you wanted to find your part He would tell you."

These students, who belonged to The Oxford Group, suggested I read a passage from the Bible early every morning, meditate on it and see if God had anything to say to me. At breakfast next day, I was asked if any messages had come and somewhat triumphantly I was able to say,

"No, nothing!"

After breakfast, I went into the washroom to clean my teeth and as I looked into the mirror, a very clear thought came to me:

"Behave decently to your father".

Not exactly the religious thought I had been waiting for, but absolutely to the point and very much needed.

My father was by then a man well into his seventies. Whenever I came back from my day at the university, he would ask:

"What did you do today, son?"

I would tell him. Then half an hour later, he would ask the same question and I would get into a rage and accuse him of only making conversation, since if he was really interested, he would have remembered the first time: the typical reaction of an impatient and self-important young man.

I apologised to my father – and so began my religious life!

Some disturbing thoughts

I continued the early morning listening sessions and some very disturbing thoughts trickled into my mind, about my relationship with a girl I had been going around with for five years, followed by some questions about money and how I conducted my financial activities. By this time, I had been seven years at the university and had come to the conclusion that I didn't have the brains for an academic life. I decided to go to Belfast, where I joined some friends, got a job as a research chemist in a food factory and worked there for the next five years.

I joined the union of the Association of Scientific Workers and became interested in the trade union movement generally. By this time, the Second World War was coming to an end and everything was still in short supply. I spent quite some time trying scientifically to make egg white without the aid of a hen; we attempted to set up a pilot plant and I loved my work at the laboratory.

Then one day I was invited to London to see a religious play; in the middle of it, I heard a voice in my ear, so loud that it seemed to come from the stage:

"You are not doing your maximum to remake the world and you are not in the right place to do it".

As soon as the show was over, I left immediately, speaking to no one and took the next boat train back to Belfast and to everyone's surprise, got back to work a day earlier than expected.

I said nothing to anyone about my experience until a friend, who had been with me in London, returned to Belfast and asked where I had got to after the show, as he had been looking out for me. So I had to tell him. After much soul-searching, I went to my boss and told him that I had the thought to resign and learn more about the trade union movement in England. He said he had invested a lot in me, with an eye to the future, and if I ever wanted to return to the factory, I could do so. His parting gift to me was a gold watch; sadly, his hopes for the future were ill-founded as six months later the firm went bankrupt.

'Set the docks ablaze for Christ'

I arrived in England in 1950, the year there was a nationwide docker's strike, which was reported to have cost Britain as much as it had received in Marshall Aid that year. The cause of the strike was over the Canadian ship, the *Beaverbrae*, and it had been well planned by the communists, who had declared the ship 'black', which meant no dockers could work on unloading it anywhere.

However, the day I arrived in London I went to a small gathering of trade unionists in the evening and heard a lady from Tate and Lyle's sugar factory saying that she had been at an international conference in Switzerland and on the train on the way back home, had the powerful conviction to go back to London and 'set the docks ablaze for Christ'. I immediately thought I would like to have a part in that.

But I knew nothing about the docks or the sea, other than that whenever I was at sea, going to the Isle of Man on holiday, or crossing to Holyhead, I was always very seasick! I had even once been sick while the boat was still tied up at the pier! Anyway, I went to stay with a vicar who had a parish on the Old Kent Road and had some dockers in his church. The vicar drove me around and showed me the Thames and the docks. Then I noticed that whenever dockers leaders' names were reported in the press, they were Irish!

We began to visit these men and one of the things I found out was that they seemed to take an interest in other countries, probably because the ships they worked on came from all over the world. So whenever people came to work with us in London from abroad, we would bring them down with us to the dockers' homes.

A steep and rapid learning curve

I soon discovered that I was on a steep and rapid learning curve. The industry was very diverse and I had to discover the difference between the various unions. There was a lot of jealousy and competition between them. Who was a docker and who was a stevedore? There were the crane drivers, another race of men, and then the aristocrats of the docks, the Watermen, Lightermen, Tugmen and Bargemen's Union. And, of course, the Transport and General Workers and the National Amalgamated Stevedores and Dockers Unions.

I gradually mastered all this and began to meet and befriend the leaders of these unions. Then there were the unofficial leaders, who by and large led the strikes! The official leaders had a standard approach to the strikes that were led by the unofficial leaders:

"Go back to work, stop the violence and then we will negotiate and deal with the problem" to which the unofficial leaders replied,

"You deal with the problem, then we will go back to work and stop the violence."

The communists, of course, manipulated the situation for their own purposes, so workers with genuine problems often found themselves exploited.

A sense of hope that they were not alone

If you could give men a sense of hope that they were not alone, then sound men would sometimes have the courage to stand up and be counted. One man who did this was Charlie Stebbing, of the Stevedores Union. He got up in a mass meeting and said,

Eric on the right with friends in the docks

"I don't think this strike is right, it's for political purposes".

When the vote was taken, the decision was not to strike.

This did not mean that men like Stebbing fought less hard for the rights of the workers or had given in to the employers: it meant they were not going to be used or exploited. At one point, a friend of mine, who was the boss of one of the old craft unions, with a left-leaning reputation, told me that he had been at a reception at the Russian Embassy in London, where a top Communist official said to him that our work in the docks had "done more damage to the Communist cause than anyone had ever done".

Attacks and failures

However, we were also attacked and smeared from all sides. I remember the shock of reading a headline in a national Sunday tabloid 'Oxford Groupers Condemned' with a statement by a leading official of the largest union in the country, the Transport and General Workers. Our main 'crime' was supposed to be that because we met with the unofficial leaders, we were encouraging them to believe they were somebody!

Of course, we had failures, too. One memorable one was Joe, whose wife Rose was Irish. As a family, they became quite interested in what we were up to. Joe would speak at various public meetings we arranged in the dock area, and on one occasion he went to Oxford to speak at a meeting of undergraduates about his change. Unfortunately, while he had become more honest since meeting us and had stopped bribing the police at the dock gates, he hadn't quit taking stuff out himself! One morning, a police sergeant came to the barge Joe was working on and discovered 94 cigarette lighters on his person.

Later, he told us that he didn't know how he did it but he leaped up out of the barge and struck the sergeant: he was grateful that he had thrown down his dockers hook before he jumped up, otherwise he might have killed the wretched man. He got three years in Exeter gaol and I used to drive Rose and his family to visit him. Rose was wonderful: when I first heard about his arrest, I went down to see them at their home in Limehouse, near one of the docks there.

Joe told me he was very ashamed – but he had not done it. He got quite angry when I told him I didn't believe him. Then Rose said, 'Joe!' and that was that: powerful people, wives! As history records, the dockers strike was eventually settled, but at enormous cost.

After four years in London, the time came for me to move on, so move on I did, although I returned to London later.

To Australia

In 1954, Australian friends invited me to their country and I really enjoyed my five years there: they have a relaxed view of life, not taking themselves too seriously, but having a deep love for their country and its destiny. I learnt a lot, while continuing my work with dockers. One of the men I got to know was Jim Healy, who was born in Manchester of Irish parents and was one of the leading Teamsters of Australia and also head of the dockworkers union, who are known as 'wharfies'.

One of the young 'wharfies' I met was Jim Beggs. He had bought a plot of land in a very respectable area of Melbourne, where he had put up a garden shed in which he and his wife Tui lived. He worked on the docks until he had saved up enough to buy building materials and he then took time off to build the house in stages. Jim's next-door neighbour happened to be Tom Uren, who was a Port employer and he was very impressed with Jim's industry. Tom invited Jim and his wife Tui to come for tea: they got talking about the Port. Tom said he wanted to see the Port different and that there ought to be new relationships between management and dockers, to which Jim naturally agreed. Tom then said that he had found that 'if you wanted things to be different, you had to start with yourself' and he suggested to Jim that he take a little time to think about it all.

'Daylight Saving'

When Jim and Tui went home, the first thing Jim saw was a clock on a shelf. Every time a new car was unloaded, the dockers picked the clock out of the car, if they could. So next morning, Jim went to the foreman and told him about the clock which he had stolen and had now decided to return. The foremen passed him on to someone higher up the management chain. However, it seems it was 'too hot to handle', so finally, Jim was sent to see the boss. "Why have you done this?" asked the boss. Jim told him that he wanted to try to do something about the spirit in the Port and that he had to start with himself.

Instead of sacking him, which Jim and Tui had feared, the boss thanked Jim and said, "Yes, we miss a lot of these clocks!" When Jim's 'wharfie' pals heard this story, they nick-named him 'Daylight saving' because he put the clock back! After some years, Jim was made Chairman of the union in the Port and finally became National Chairman of the Waterside Workers of Australia.

Jim's father was born in Dromore, Co. Antrim, and when Jim first visited Ireland, he decided to see if there were any relatives left in Dromore. He went into the first shop he saw and told the girl behind the counter that he came from Australia and asked her if there were any Beggs in the town, to which she replied, "Yes, at least 50, and I'm one of them!" So he met up with his uncle's family and since then has visited and stayed with them several times, with his wife Tui, and we have kept in touch ever since, when he gives me the latest news of Australia.

To the U.S.A.

It was early January 1951 that I first visited New York briefly, when a friend took me up to the top of the Rockefeller Centre. Looking out across the city, I fell in love with it there and then. It was almost ten years later before I was able to spend any extended time in America and then I spent three years there.

In America, dockers are known as longshoremen and the union is the International Longshoreman's Association (ILA). At that time, Irishmen led the union. Passenger liners came into Manhattan, where the Irish were in control, but the main cargo-handling centre was in Brooklyn and there it was the Italians who were in charge.

I had got to know the Irish and mentioned to one of them that I'd like to get to know the men in Brooklyn. He replied,

"Well then, you'll have to get permission from Tony Anastasia. Otherwise one day you will disappear and the next day you'll be found floating face down in the water."

The Anastasia family was a large one. One brother, Umberto, was head of 'Murder Incorporated', a Mafia business run for profit – it was said that they

Dockers, New York, 1950s

had murdered at least two hundred: the more important you were, the higher the price paid to murder you. Another brother was a priest in the Bronx. Umberto made the mistake of going regularly to the same barber for a shave and one morning, two gunmen came in while he was sitting in the chair and sprayed bullets into him.

Tough Tony

I decided to try and see Tony Anastasia – Tough Tony, as he was called. So I rang him up and said I'd bring along a New Yorker, Scotty Macfarlane, with me and told Tony that we were connected with an organisation called Moral Re-Armament (MRA). I think he agreed to meet us because he was so surprised at the prospect of meeting with anyone connected with anything moral!

He turned out to be a man who looked more like a barber than a docker, with brushed-back silver grey hair and a natty black suit. He seemed very pleasant. Shortly afterwards, a delegation of Brazilian dockers from Rio de Janeiro arrived in New York and I rang Tony, who agreed to meet them, along with a number of his union officials. One of these was a black man called Fred

Small. Looking back, I think Tony only agreed to meet the Rio dockers because he hoped to establish a drugs run with Latin America, using the Dockers' Union.

As a matter of principle, the Irish would not allow blacks in their union branches but as Tony needed to get his numbers up, he made them welcome. It turned out that Fred Small, who was anything but small, being an enormous man over 6 feet tall and very strong, was the organiser of all the blacks in the docks and was National Vice-President of the Negro-American Labour Council. I think Tony was warned by the Mafia to have nothing further to do with MRA, because he told Fred later not to see us any more: however, Fred paid no attention.

'The cream coloured Chrysler'

Fred drove a cream coloured Chrysler, which he loved: he said it was his home. If we wanted to meet with Fred, we would keep our eyes fixed on the Chrysler and sure enough, he would eventually turn up. One day I was sitting in a café, watching the Chrysler out of the window and waiting for Fred, when a big black Cadillac drove up to the union office and Tony Anastasia got out. His chauffeur was busy getting something out of the car when he saw me and came over to the café. He rapped on the window, beckoning me to come out. Everyone in the café went silent: they knew who he was and so did I. He was Manuel Leopold, Tony's gunman, among his other duties. I went out and he said,

"What are you doing here?"

"Waiting for a friend," I replied.

"What?" he said.

"Waiting for a friend," I repeated.

"All right," he said and walked away. Still trembling in my shoes somewhat, I returned to the café and not long after, Fred came out of the union office and we joined him. He told me later that Manuel had told him I was outside waiting for him.

'Put away' for a spell

When he was a young teenager, Fred was travelling as a passenger in a stolen car, which was stopped by the police. The driver got away but Fred was shot in the leg and he was 'put away' for a spell. "I went in an amateur and came out a professional" was his comment. His father was a minister in a small church, but lost his position as a result of having a son who had been in trouble. As a result, Fred was turned out of his home and went to live with a prostitute, for whom he stole 'to order'. He graduated to driving a taxi in New York before finally becoming a foreman at the Brooklyn docks.

I went through many adventures with Fred, as I did with the Irish. The head of the Longshoremen's Union in America, Teddy Gleason, was a New York born Irishman, whose father was from Leitrim and mother was from Tipperary. The union featured in the famous film 'On the Waterfront' with Marlon Brando. Teddy disputed the realism of the movie, not on the basis of the murders but because a longshoreman was shown throwing a beer can at a priest. "That would never happen," said Gleason.

To Killarney – and back to Belfast!

My story now goes forward in time to when I was living in Northern Ireland in the early 1970s. I heard that Teddy Gleason was bringing a group from his union to a conference in Dublin, which he said was as cheap as flying to Miami. One of the delegates was my friend Fred Small from Brooklyn. I was in Belfast when I heard about this visit, so I went down to Dublin to meet Fred; I suggested to him that instead of going to Killarney for a 'booze up' after the conference, which the rest of the delegation planned, he might come with me to Belfast, where he would meet some interesting people.

He accepted my invitation and we set off that evening, with Fred sitting beside me in my car. We were stopped at the border by a soldier who asked me for my driving licence. Fred, being black, was not noticed, until he opened his mouth, when his white teeth suddenly appeared in this black space! The soldier jumped back in alarm and naturally enough, got angry and demanded,

"Who is he?"

Fortunately, there had been a very good photo of Fred in that morning's *Irish Times* in a story about the Longshoremen's conference: because he appeared in the paper, he must be respectable! So we were waved on our way without further ado. I had warned Fred not to take his gun with him but to leave it behind in his suitcase, which was to be sent with the delegation's luggage to Shannon via Killarney.

After three eventful days together in Belfast, I drove Fred and a friend to a new hotel near Killarney, which had not yet been officially opened, to join up with the rest of the New York delegation. As soon as we walked into the busy throng of people in the hotel lobby, my friend turned to me and said,

"My God, there's the high command of the IRA".

It turned out that the Longshoremen were the only guests in the hotel at that point. While we were standing there with Fred, wondering what to do next, the top man from Derry, who knew me, came over and greeted me.

"What are you doing here, Eric?"

I hastily introduced him to "my friend Fred Small" who was clearly not an agent of the police or the army! So the man went back across the room to his colleagues and we could see them consulting together, and then he came back to ask me where I was living now.

"Belfast," I replied and swiftly added "but I'm going to Canada next week" which happened to be the truth!

That seemed to satisfy them and eventually they left the hotel. I asked Fred if he would mind going out of the front door of the hotel to see if they really had left and weren't just waiting round the corner for us. As soon as we got the all clear, we made our farewells and made off as quick as we could to Killarney, where we played golf for a few days to recover from the shock!

So my friend Fred, an African American from the heart of the Brooklyn docks in New York, was directly connected with the two most frightening episodes of my life! A year later, when I met up with him again in New York, he told me he had been very relieved to get back home to the relative safety of the Brooklyn Mafia! Then he said, "You know, Eric, I learnt more about race relations in those three days I spent with you in Belfast than I did in all my life in the United States. I thought prejudice was about colour."

Chapter 2

NEXT ARE FOUR stories that were sent to us on hearing of Eric's death in Belfast on 20th October 2014 aged 95.

The first of these tributes is from Gordon Wise, an Australian married to Marjory, a Scot. At that point in his life, Gordon had adopted London as their sphere of work, in those difficult years for post-war Britain. It is probably not generally know or remembered today, for instance, that the UK Labour government had to bring in bread rationing *after* the war had ended, such was the shortage of grain.

An Australian's perspective, from Gordon and Marjory Wise

When Eric arrived in England in 1950, we worked together, along with others, in meeting the London dockers and their unions, the complications of which Eric describes vividly in the first chapter.

One of the first men we met was Tom Keep, who had been President of the National Amalgamated Stevedores and Dockers' Union. For 22 years he had been a leading advocate of the Communist Party, (CP) for which he spoke passionately from every public platform he could. However, thanks largely due to several months of Eric's care for him and his family, Tom broke with the Party and accepted the ideas that Eric stood for and believed in, which in essence was that there is a better way for mankind and society than the ideology of 'the dictatorship of the proletariat', and this better way is 'God control, if you go at it hammer and tongs', which appealed to Tom's pioneering spirit.

However, one day we had word from Tom's wife Kitty that he was going to re-join the CP. As Tom was such a spell-binding speaker, this would soon become known throughout the docks and be used by his enemies and ours to attack what we were trying to do in the docks. Eric asked me to accompany him to visit Tom to see what we could do. Kitty was home but Tom was out. We prayed together – and Tom walked through the door holding two pet rabbits given him by a friend!

"You see", said Tom, "I couldn't very well go to the Party meeting carrying these rabbits, so decided to come home".

We asked him how communism works, at which point his wife Kitty called out from the kitchen: "It doesn't bloody well work around here!"

In time, with Eric's faithfulness and understanding, Tom changed his mind and was back in action with what was his true self, battling for the right ideas for British industry, beyond the sterile class war philosophy so much in vogue then.

Eric chaired many meetings in Canning Town Hall in the 1950s. He knew the area like the back of his hand and some of the personalities and their histories through and through. However, it was not an easy battle and at one point a friend of Eric's, Albert Timothy and some of his associates, were charged with conspiracy by the police. Timothy, known as 'Timmo', was chairman of what was known as an unofficial dockers committee, and clearly it was a trumped up charge by his opponents. I went with Eric to the Old Bailey Court to hear the case against them and Timothy gave us a wave from the dock. At one point in the proceedings a policeman read out a statement which referred to MRA and the Judge interrupted saying, "What is the MRA?" The policeman replied, "The Moral Re-Armament, m'lud". The charges were dropped.

I remember visiting Timmo another day with Eric, during a port dispute which was threatening a major stoppage. We had a time of quiet reflection and Timmo's thought was, which he proclaimed loud and clear, "'old yer 'orses – no strike."

At that time, the moving spirit of the dockers was a communist named Ted Dickens and one day when we visited Timmo at his home, to our surprise we found Ted there; I think we gave as good as we got in the ensuing vigorous discussion!

London

Eric in Australia and my visit to the UK, from Jim and Tui Beggs

How well we remember Eric's time in Australia. He was here at an important time in my life and the life of my industry. I was a young dock worker and I quickly got a sense of his love for the docks and those of us who worked in them.

The Melbourne waterfront was in turmoil then and I had opted out of getting involved. He lived next door to my wife Tui and me and he helped us to seek God's guidance each morning. This led to us getting involved: he had more faith in us that we could be used to change the waterfront than we did, and he would come down to the port at least once a week to meet my gang. His constancy, care and comradeship led to me building a team in the port of Melbourne and later becoming the National President of my union.

Some years later, in 1968, Eric invited me to the UK, where he had arranged for me to meet some of his mates from the ports; this included London, Liverpool, Newcastle, Hull, Southampton, Tilbury, Grangemouth, Bristol and Avonmouth and the Clyde in Glasgow, and of course his beloved Belfast. In the six weeks I was in the UK I met over a hundred; they were not only dockers, seafarers and boilermakers, there were Lord Mayors, Councillors, Managing Directors of steamship companies, Members of Parliament, Labour and Conservative, and Lord Simon, Chairman of the Port of London Authority, and Jack Dash, chairman of the unofficial strike committee in London.

Whether you came from the Left or the Right, it didn't matter to Eric, these were his friends. They were all meetings of substance, not just about the problems on the docks, but wider issues troubling the world today, unemployment, family break-down, the starving millions. Eric's words to each one we met were simple, "If you want to see the world different, the place to start is with yourself."

On a lighter note, Eric's passion for golf worried me a bit at times! He used to practice his chipping shots over on the local park in east London where he lived, at about 8am every day until the local Councillor told him it was illegal. Eric thanked him, picked up his 7 iron and golf balls and went home. The next day he was back there at 6am practising again!

He got a lot of his golf equipment from exchanging Green Stamps at certain petrol stations and he knew where he could get the most Green Stamps! As I travelled with him all over the UK, there were times when I thought we would have to push his car to get to the petrol station − he'd

Jim Beggs looking across Victoria Dock in Melbourne, 2013, 42 years later

squeeze every last drop out of his little Morris Minor! And when we later visited my family in Northern Ireland, how I enjoyed playing golf with the three musketeers, Eric and his friends Roddy Evans and David Hume. Eric certainly left his mark on our country; he was a bloke who not only loved his country but the whole world.

Melbourne, Australia

Working with Eric, from Alec Porter

Eric and I first met when we were at Trinity College, Dublin, where I did agriculture and Eric studied chemistry and medicine. We went our different ways after graduating, and our paths crossed again in 1949, after I had spent a year or so among the miners of the Welsh valleys. Then at a particularly low point in my life, I had an unexpected and welcome encounter with Eric who asked me if I would like to come and work with him meeting with dockers in London. I decided to accept Eric's invitation and so began a new and exciting chapter in my life.

Happily for us, we were invited to stay with the Rev Ian Miller, in his Vicarage at New Cross, south east London. He had been meeting dockers for some time, and one of the first men he introduced us to was George Hern, Secretary of the Docker's branch of the National Amalgamated Stevedores and Dockers Union (NASDU). One day when visiting George in his home, Eric and I found him in great distress. He told us his wife Ida had left him, taking their two daughters, along with some of the furniture.

We did our best (as single men!) to calm him. That summer George went with Eric to Caux, the international MRA centre in Switzerland. There, George got a different perspective for his life and made the important decision to 'quit the booze', which had clearly been the reason for the marriage breakdown. He told us that one day on his daughter's birthday he'd arrived home clearly drunk, found some friends there for a birthday party and had ordered the guests out of the house: that was the tipping point for his family, who later cleared off too.

By chance Ian Miller met Ida in the street one day and discovered she was living quite close by with her sister, with the two girls. As George had clearly changed his habits, Ian and his wife Dorothea invited George and Ida to the Vicarage, along with the two youngsters and they met there on several Sunday afternoons for tea. Ida made it clear that the family could not return to their present home, as the memories were so bad, so they decided to move to a new home and live together as a family again.

Another man Ian Miller had introduced us to was Dan Hurley. He also went to Caux in the summer of 1950, where Eric arranged for him to meet Frank Buchman. Dan was an official of NASDU and politically was left-leaning but not a communist. However, through his trade union work, he became involved in the *Beaverbrae* strike. This Canadian ship had been declared 'black' by the communists in Canada before the ship had left that country, with the result that no dockers could work on the ship in the UK. This was the costly strike Eric refers to in his talk in the first chapter.

After getting home from his visit to Caux, Dan Hurley wrote to Frank Buchman: 'My outlook has certainly adopted an entirely new aspect, and how much easier it has become to see the other fellow's point of view, and not to be forever prepared to ram home the very aggressive doctrine which has been part of my policy for such a long time'.

The thing that always struck me about Eric was his courage and single-mindedness in everything he did. Working with Eric was a fascinating and invigorating experience!

Glasgow

'A letter from Eric that changed my life', from Ivan Poulton

More than 30 years ago an IRA bomb killed nine young British soldiers. My wife Maisie and I were then 12,000 miles away in New Zealand. Initially thoughts of loved ones at home who might have been close by crossed our minds. Then as an Englishman who had fought for my country in the Second World War, I was filled with anger. But an unexpected thought struck me: "You are part of the problem".

Suddenly an image of airline passengers appeared in my mind's eye; they were waiting in London to board a charter aircraft for the conferences at Caux. As the man responsible for the allocation of seats, I had substituted a newcomer in place of one of the waiting passengers at nearly the last moment; the displaced person was a mild-mannered man from Belfast, Dick Loughlin. My involuntary excuse was that in my view, the newcomer was more important for the conference. But Dick was furious. Upset and surprised by his very public outburst, I rebuked Dick for his anger. Any idea of apology for what I had done never entered my head. We parted the worst of friends.

This had happened away back in the early 1950s, but clearly, I had remembered it in detail over the decades! So the thought that if I was part of the problem, this made me conscious of needing to make amends. But it was by then in the 1980s, so I wrote to my Irish friend, Eric, telling him the story, as by this time Dick Loughlin had died. Eric wrote back, in a letter that I treasure:

"I am sure Dick would now forgive you. It is most interesting, that facet of English character. We are up against it now in the present civil war in the North. Westminster says, 'Stop the violence and then we will consider the rights and the wrongs of the case, but we must first put down the men of violence to prove that crime does not pay'. It has always seemed more logical to me that if what was wrong was put right, then perhaps it would be easier to stop the violence."

For me and Maisie, Eric's letter led to our first visit to Northern Ireland in 1987. This has since led to nearly thirty years of search for a way that Irish and English, friends together, can use our long-troubled past to lead to a new teamwork, with God's grace and guidance. This could give hope and practical help to populations struggling in conflicts elsewhere. Eric's letter, all those years ago, gave us a new and focused life purpose. We can never be grateful enough, and it led to many other visits across the water, staying with different friends there and always having lively chats with Eric and others, like George Dallas, Roddy Evans and Jim Lynn.

Fortunately for both Ireland and England, the Good Friday Agreement of 1998, the public apology by Prime Minister David Cameron in 2010 for the killings of 'Bloody Sunday' in 1972 and the historic visit of the Queen to Dublin, followed by the State visit to London by the Irish President, and Prince Charles' speech when he visited Mullaghmore, in Co. Sligo in May 2015 are signs that the wrongs of the past are in the course of being put right. A sentence in Eric's letter stands out: 'One does envy the chance England has to change the world'.

London

Ivan and Maisie Poulton, Eric, Ruth and George Dallas

Chapter 3

ERIC TOLD ME this moving story long after the event, when we were both living in Northern Ireland:

After Eric had decided to end the five year relationship with his girlfriend, it was not long before he got an invitation to her wedding to another bloke! He decided to accept the invitation, out of courtesy; however, when he got to the door of the church, he couldn't go in. His emotions went deeper and were more shattering than he had realised, so he turned on his heel and left, without a word.

What was he to do next, in his confusion and anguish? Then Eric remembered a churchman who had recently visited Trinity College, whom he had met in the rooms of his friend Roddy Evans. This was the Archdeacon Gordon Hannon, whose view of his Christian calling seemed to Eric to be far more relevant and fascinating than anything he had been involved in up to that point. Since he knew the Hannon address in Ligoneil, Belfast, he got in touch with them and decided to head north.

When he arrived at the house, he found that the family lunch was over, but Gordon's wife Hilda welcomed him warmly into her kitchen and fed him, but perhaps more importantly, noticing he was somewhat downcast, asked him what was troubling him – and out poured his story. At that moment she must have been like the mother Eric never knew as he was growing up.

The upshot was that he was invited to stay and he got to know Gordon and Hilda well, along with their family of five boys and their daughter Ruth. Eric then found the job in a chemistry research laboratory that he describes in Chapter 1. Five years later, he decided to leave the security of the job he loved and head out on his odyssey across the continents.

All of twenty years later, after he had returned again to Northern Ireland, Eric was driving south with his friend Father Christopher McCarthy to a meeting in Dublin and he was telling this story to his friend as they drove along. He described how he had been struck by the breadth of vision of Archdeacon Hannon's talk when he had visited them at Trinity earlier. When he had suggested to the Dublin students that one day any of them might find themselves 'responsible for the work on the west coast of America' Eric told Father McCarthy that he didn't even realise America had a west coast!

Then Eric thought to himself that Gordon Hannon was someone who has taken on the task of remaking the world in Christ's image, and one day he must meet up with him and find out more. Father McCarthy asked Eric what the difference had been between the folk in Dublin in the Oxford Group and those in Belfast, to which Eric replied, "In Dublin we were largely concerned with the necessary job of perfecting our souls, but we hadn't considered the equally needed challenge to remake the world".

Gordon Hannon

Gordon Hannon was born in 1890 in Athy, Co. Kildare. After graduating from Trinity College Dublin, as a young priest, he went north to the Trinity Mission in Belfast. Later he was Rector of Shankill parish in Lurgan, Co. Armagh, one of the largest Church of Ireland parishes in Ireland, and was appointed Archdeacon of Dromore.

In 1932, unexpectedly, he was invited by the Anglican Dean of Manchester Cathedral to come to a conference there called 'A School of Life for Clergy' run by The Oxford Group, which he accepted. When Gordon told them of his concerns about the future of Ireland, a friend suggested to him that if he wanted to see things different in his country he might consider starting with himself by taking Christ's Sermon on the Mount seriously in his own life. He accepted this challenge and his change was soon apparent, both in his parish work with people and his wife and family.

When Frank Buchman launched Moral Re-Armament in 1939, Gordon Hannon felt he had a calling to join this challenge and should free himself from his parish responsibilities by resigning so that he could take on the wider needs of the nation. He sought the advice of his Archbishop, Dr John Gregg, and asked the Archbishop whether it would be worthwhile to attempt to enlist perhaps half a dozen of Ireland's leaders to give their lives to God for the sake of their country, to which the Archbishop replied vigorously, "It would be worth it if only one or two did such a thing." He then gave Gordon his blessing for the venture, although he regretted the church could not support him financially.

Stepped out in faith

Gordon and his wife Hilda, with their family, then stepped out in faith, without salary. To their great gratitude and thanksgiving, this was richly rewarded by the generosity of many who supported them. A mill owner offered his then unused large 13 bedroomed house, Wolfhill, on the outskirts of Belfast, to Gordon for a rent of £100 a year, plus free electricity from the mill – and with two trout streams for fishing! From this base, Gordon reached out to local civic and political leaders, and a great variety of people rallied to his initiative.

Over the following years, Gordon made contact with many personalities throughout Ireland, one of whom was Maude Gonne McBride, an English born suffragette who was won over to Irish nationalism by the plight of evicted people in the land wars. She actively agitated for Irish home rule and her husband John McBride was one of those executed for his part in the 1916 uprising. When Gordon visited her, she was writing a book about the current Irish situation, and she told him she was in the middle of a chapter dealing with the Orange Order and giving it a thorough slating. Gordon then told her that he himself had been a member of the Order; at once she ran out of the room and summoned her family so that they could see and talk to 'a real live Orangeman'!

Another of Gordon's friends was Lord Hugh Beresford, who was a prominent member of the Anglo-Irish community. Gordon arranged a visit for Hugh to meet Eamon de Valera, whom they visited together in

Dublin. More than forty years later, *The Irish Times* in March 1984 carried this report:

'Father Michael MacGriel S.J. revealed that President De Valera told him of an Anglo-Irish peer who asked to meet him around the beginning of the Second World War. His visitor told the President that he regretted very much the hostility between the Anglo-Irish Ascendancy and those who set up the new Irish State and their passivity in relation to public life. He promised that after the war he would offer his services to building up the Irish State.

The impact of this noble gesture so impressed de Valera that he felt that he, for his part, would welcome such support. Unfortunately the peer was killed in action while serving with Lord Mountbatten on HMS Kelly when the destroyer was sunk by enemy action in 1942 but his offer had a lasting effect on de Valera.'

When Gordon Hannon died in 1978 aged 87, the *County Down Spectator* wrote a full appreciation of his life and work, which included this paragraph:

'In 1949, when the Congress of Europe was launched at The Hague, Eamon de Valera asked Archdeacon Hannon to go to the Congress and speak for the North. The Archdeacon took with him Mr Fred Thompson, a Unionist MP in Belfast, and in the following year they both attended the Council of Europe at Strasbourg.'

'The Forgotten Factor'

In 1946 Dr Frank Buchman came from America to a war-torn Europe with a large team and the industrial play 'The Forgotten Factor'. The campaign began in Belfast, where the ground had been thoroughly prepared by Gordon Hannon and his team. The theatre was packed to capacity for three weeks and the foundations were laid for the progress of the work in the years to come.

After Belfast, 'The Forgotten Factor' did an extensive tour of the mining towns of Great Britain, and here I add a personal note, as Gordon and Hilda's daughter Ruth played a teenager in the cast – and twenty years later became my wife!

After the tour of Great Britain, the cast went to Caux, the international conference centre in Switzerland, where Dr Frank Buchman asked Gordon and Hilda Hannon, who were also delegates at the conference, if he could

David and Ruth Hume with daughter Frances Hume.

include their daughter Ruth in a visit he was going to make (with 200 others!) to Sri Lanka and India. So Ruth spent her 21st birthday in Srinagar in Kashmir, India, a truly memorable experience, and in later years our daughter Frances has visited India and Sri Lanka several times.

Chapter 4

A brief historical review, by Dr Roddy Evans

The following is an attempt to account for the movement of history that culminated in thirty years of civil war in Northern Ireland.

From the earliest years, the involvement of the English Crown in Ireland was always at 'one remove'. The oligarchy that ruled Ireland on behalf of the Crown was English until the sixteenth century. The historian W.E.H. Lecky wrote 'The English rule was concentrated in the narrow limits of the Pale. Like a spearhead in a living body, it inflamed all around it and deranged every vital function.'

As Europe's seafaring empires rose and sea-lanes opened up, England's fears of Catholic France and Spain sharpened: thus the Reformation was an opportunity for the English to maintain control of Catholic Ireland. Over a period of time, the definition of the ruling oligarchy ceased to be solely English and became also Protestant. This ruling elite established itself in Ireland and was subsequently known as the 'Protestant Ascendancy'.

At the close of the eighteenth century, the revolutionary ideas that spawned the American War of Independence and the French Revolution ignited the 1798 revolution in Ireland. This was inspired by the Protestant leader Wolfe Tone and the United Irishmen and the aim of this rebellion by Irish Catholics and Presbyterians was to overthrow the Ascendancy and usher in a more just government. The subsequent crushing of the rebellion was followed by the Act of Union in 1800, establishing the United Kingdom of Great Britain and Ireland. Vestiges of that Act are still extant and lie at the root of the continuing situation in Northern Ireland. The appalling potato famine of the 1840s led to a million deaths and a further million went into exile, mainly to America. The trauma of that event sharpened Irish nationalist feeling and this was reflected throughout the Irish diaspora, especially in the

U.S.A. In the mid-nineteenth century, just before the great famine, Daniel O'Connell the Liberator attempted to repeal the act of Union, without success. But he did succeed in achieving Catholic emancipation reluctantly conceded by an English government led by the Duke of Wellington.

Under the Act of Union, the governance of Ireland was the responsibility of the Westminster parliament, and the Protestant Ascendancy was the means of that governance. W.E. Gladstone was the first English politician to realise that such a system of government was far from satisfactory and he announced, 'We aim at the destruction of the system of the Ascendancy, which is still there, like a great tree of noxious growth, lifting its head and poisoning the land as far as its shadow can extend.' Edmund Burke described the Protestant Ascendancy as 'pure and perfect malice . . . as to religion, it has nothing to do with the proceedings.' However, Lecky wrote, 'Of all class tyrannies, the most odious is the one which rests on religious distinctions and is envenomed by religious animosities.'

From 1886 to 1918, the Westminster parliament was in continuous turmoil, as Parnell, leader of the Irish Party in the House of Commons, and his successors, attempted to secure a Home Rule Bill to establish an Irish parliament in Dublin. Three Bills were introduced but all failed. Their failures fuelled the Irish physical force tradition that led directly to the Easter Rising in 1916 and the Anglo-Irish war from 1919 to 1921.

This was followed by the Anglo-Irish Treaty, which in turn sparked the bloody civil war across Ireland. The six counties of Northern Ireland were offered devolution, while remaining part of the United Kingdom and this became the Government of Ireland Act of 1921. Austin Chamberlain, one of the signatories of the Anglo-Irish Treaty was reported as saying, 'Northern Ireland is an illogical and indefensible compromise.' He realised that the constitutional acts passed at the time were temporary compromises. However, they did succeed in getting the 'troublesome' Irish question out of Westminster affairs for the next fifty years.

The temporary nature of the arrangements was bound to lead to change. So why did it take fifty years before these changes finally began? One obvious reason was that from its inception the system did not facilitate the growth of a Catholic nationalist middle class. It was not until the 1947 Butler Education

Act in Northern Ireland that both young Catholics and Protestants could benefit from university education. However, the eventual explosion in Northern Ireland was triggered by the Catholic university students' demand for civil rights, justice and equality in 1968. This coincided with student riots in America and France.

Again, when the situation descended to civil war, why did it last for thirty years? Two factors suggest a possible explanation. Firstly, 1970 saw the election of a Conservative government returned to power in Westminster, which reversed the previous Labour government's policy of reform, and attempted to deal with the situation strictly on a 'law and order' basis. This policy merely exacerbated the conflict. Secondly, in Dublin there was a serious crisis threatening the stability of the state, in that senior government Ministers appeared to be attempting to supply arms to the Catholic nationalists in Northern Ireland, for use in a possible 'doomsday' situation. This led to the Arms Trials and as a result, Dublin recoiled from any involvement in the gathering storm in the North. Garret Fitzgerald was one of the chief architects of keeping the Southern state out of the conflict.

A watershed in history

In the context of the thirty years of conflict, there are a number of important landmarks. The first was the use by the British government of internment without trial, followed by the British army shooting dead fourteen unarmed civilians in Derry in 1972. These events ended the civil rights campaign and turned it into an armed conflict. The British government then tried to 'criminalise' it, which led to ten prisoners fasting to death in 1982 in reaction.

The signing of the Anglo-Irish Agreement in 1985 by Prime Ministers Garret Fitzgerald and Margaret Thatcher was an attempt to halt the rise of Sinn Fein, which it conspicuously failed to do. However, the Agreement did place Dublin as a partner with London in planning the way forward in Northern Ireland. The earlier entry of Ireland and the UK into the EEC in 1973 had played a part in this development.

It was the disastrous consequences of the Remembrance Day bomb in Enniskillen in 1987 that was the watershed in the armed conflict. This intensified the then secret talks in search of peace, which later involved U.S.A.

President Ronald Reagan urging Margaret Thatcher to conclude the Anglo-Irish Agreement, which she did, against all her natural instincts.

However, the involvement of President Bill Clinton from 1994 was more significant and his important decisions were:

- granting a visa to Gerry Adams to enter the U.S.A. against strong opposition from the British government

- moving the Irish question from the State Department Foreign Affairs to the National Security Council in the White House

- the appointment of Jean Kennedy Smith as U.S. Ambassador in Dublin

- appointing Senator George Mitchell as the U.S.A.'s Special Envoy in Northern Ireland.

All this led directly to the signing of the 1998 Good Friday Agreement in Belfast by all the political parties involved, confirmed by referenda in both the North and the South.

Looking at the history of the last thirty years or so in retrospect, it is clear that when the campaign for civil rights began in 1968, both Dublin and London failed to see the omens and when the storm broke, both governments were totally unprepared. This was more serious for London, as Westminster had jurisdiction over the Province.

Four years earlier, in 1964, a Labour government, under Harold Wilson, had come to power after thirteen years in opposition. It was a government beset with problems. Paul Arthur, Professor of Politics at the University of Ulster, writes:

'In all their difficult circumstances, domestic and external, it was not surprising that initially Northern Ireland was regarded as a side-show, which Richard Crossman recorded in his diary 'From the point of view of government, it has its advantages. It has deflected attention from our own deficiencies and the mess of the pound. We have now got into something we can hardly mismanage.'

A 'paranocracy'

Mismanage it they did. The British government was psychologically and politically ill-equipped for the coming storm. One must remember the degree to which Northern Ireland was not a democracy but a 'paranocracy' in which, as Ken Heskin, Lecturer in Psychology at the University of Ulster writes, 'the basis of power was the successful appeal to paranoid fears in the Protestant electorate about the political, social, philosophical and military potential of their Catholic neighbours. This was impervious to economic and social failures, impervious to logical and political rebuttal, and fuelled simply by regular doses of paranoia at appropriate moments in the social and political calendar. What led to the collapse of the old order was the sustained attention from outside.'

The closing thirty-two years of the twentieth century witnessed dramatic developments in the long, complex and often tragic relationship between the people of the two islands off the north-west coast of Europe. Many other players were progressively drawn into the drama, from Europe, Africa and the U.S.A. and in future years, historians will sift and analyse the details of these events, while novelists and dramatists will attempt to create their masterpieces from what was undoubtedly a watershed in history.

Chapter 5

Eric arrives back in Belfast

IN 1970, AT a point when the 'troubles' seemed to be getting worse by the day, Eric was known occasionally to *craic* "I came to do whatever I could to help – since then things have got steadily worse!" However, he gave his heart and mind to everyone he met, without judgement or condemnation, and this attitude led him into many situations and to meet many people, in the years to come.

Two friends were also there, Bill and Muriel Porter, from those early days together at Trinity College Dublin. They were joined in 1972 by Dr Roddy Evans, who had spent the previous ten years in India; he had read about the civil rights movement and the disturbances in Northern Ireland in the Indian newspapers and decided that his place was to be there. He knew or was acquainted with Eric even further back than the Trinity days, as they were both pupils at King's Hospital School in Dublin; Eric was the older, so they didn't meet socially until they both went to Trinity. Roddy recalls a brief contact when he had been discovered doing something forbidden at school and it was Eric who had administered the traditional punishment – probably banned at the school today!

Dr Winifred Hind

In Belfast, Eric was invited to stay with Dr Winifred Hind, where the Porters had been her guests throughout the 1960s, while Roddy Evans was welcomed into the home of friends he knew from earlier days, Brian and Margaret Hewitt and their two young sons James and David.

Dr Winifred Hind was an elderly widow living in a large house in 10 Broomhill Park, off the Malone Road. This was in an area of the city that people from both communities and from abroad could visit safely. Without doubt, Winifred fulfilled every requirement of a *grande dame* and was a formidable character! After graduating in 1914 from Edinburgh University as one of the first women to become a doctor, she fulfilled an earlier determination to be a missionary in China. There is no record of those days, other than that she married John Hind, a CMS Church of Ireland Bishop, who had encountered The Oxford Group in China, where Frank Buchman had earlier visited. When the Bishop retired after forty years in China, he and Winifred returned to his native heath in Belfast. Having spent the previous twenty five years in China, Belfast was a new experience for Winifred, but she remembered with affection earlier days she had spent as a medical student at the Rotunda Hospital in Dublin.

Winifred was a woman of great humanity and largeness of heart, with a lively concern and interest in other people and in events in the world around her. And she had a deep longing that her home might be used to heal the wounds of a suffering Province. Over the few remaining years of Winifred's life, Eric got to know her well and they talked over many topics. At one point, after Winifred had made a decision about what she wanted to happen to her home after she died, she asked Eric to be sure that 'the right thing would be done.'

In 1979 she died peacefully at her home, aged 90; a great English lady who fulfilled the vision she had in her early years and maintained throughout her long life. The Rector of St. Bartholomew's Church of Ireland conducted a small service for Winifred and her family and friends at her home on the 30th October. She left her home to The Oxford Group 'for the furtherance of the work of Moral Re-Armament in Ireland' but without any assets to support its upkeep and use, as these were left in trust to her two nephews.

Leslie Fox

During the 1970s and 80s a feature of life at Broomhill, as Winifred's home became known, was a regular weekly meeting of a group of older ladies, some with their husbands and others as widows, as well as a couple of bachelors, Roddy Evans and Eric Turpin! This became known as The Thursday Ladies, for want of any better description. The ladies brought their own picnic lunch, which they ate in the sitting room, while the men were treated to soup, cheese and fruit served in the dining room. This was generally followed by a gathering of all present, to discuss what was going on and get news of events elsewhere.

On one occasion, their visitor was Leslie Fox, the Treasurer of The Oxford Group in London, where its headquarters are registered as a charity in England and Wales. During the gathering which Leslie attended, the future of the fund which Winifred had initiated for the upkeep of the home was discussed. One of the ladies, Miss Molly Poston asked Leslie what guarantee the people in Belfast who wished to contribute to the fund would have that the money would be used for the work in Ireland and not just be sent to the headquarters in London. Molly's home was in Carryduff in south Belfast and she had run a small haberdashery shop there. Leslie Fox assured Molly that an arrangement could be made to cover her important point. However, Molly was very hard of hearing, with an old fashioned attached hearing aid which she had to aim by hand at anyone speaking to her. So it was not long before she asked the same question again, to which Leslie replied in precisely the same words. However, the inevitable happened yet again, with the query repeated. This time, Leslie rose from his seat and spoke loudly and clearly into the hearing device: "Cross my heart and hope to die, I hereby swear by Almighty God . . ." to deal with the problem, which happily he duly did by creating The Oxford Group Special Purposes Ireland account.

As probably only Molly knew, although some might have guessed, she intended to leave her home to The Oxford Group, always provided she was sure the proceeds would not merely end up in London. Bless her, when she died not long afterwards, she left the proceeds of the sale of her home to The Oxford Group. This ensured sufficient funds to cover the payment of all the monthly utilities bills for 10 Broomhill Park for some years ahead, something that Winifred had longed would happen.

A close friendship

A footnote to this story is that Eric and Leslie later struck up a close friendship, which in the light of the relationship between Northern Ireland, Ireland and England, became important, particularly in the efforts towards bringing about peace. As a result of a personal spiritual experience, Leslie had an exceptionally clear perception of 'the problem', which he wrote about in *The Irish Times* in Dublin in 1983 and is printed in Chapter 7.

Leslie told Eric at one point, "I have taken a lot of stick about you…" by which Leslie meant in London, where for reasons best known to themselves, some of his colleagues with whom he worked, distrusted and even despised the Irish. 'Nothing new' you might say. But in the context, it was a sad reflection of the ignorance these people preferred to remain in, rather than 'risk their necks' and reputation, so called, with their own English establishment.

Thankfully, over time and as you will read in a later chapter, a relationship was established, fortuitously by Leslie himself, who lived in Dulwich, London, at the time, and this developed into an important breakthrough into the English, thanks be to God.

Dr George Dallas

A regular visitor to Winifred's home, Dr George Dallas was an unusual person: it would not be an exaggeration to add 'exceptionally' unusual. George was born in 1922 in Ballybay, Co. Monaghan, where his father was a teacher. When Co. Monaghan did not become part of Northern Ireland, he moved his family north to Dervock, in Co. Antrim, where he got a teaching post in a church school.

When George was sixteen he contracted lung tuberculosis and he had to have regular medical treatment for the rest of his life. He had wanted to be a medical missionary but his illness prevented this. However, as a doctor, he became an expert in the care of patients with tuberculosis, frequently travelling to treat patients in hospitals across the Province and elsewhere.

Throughout his life, George had an abiding love for his Presbyterian community in Northern Ireland. He would have described himself as a supporter of Wolfe Tone and the United Irishmen of the 1798 rebellion. However, like many Presbyterians, he was not keen on the Anglican Church of Ireland, especially those from the south of Ireland.

When Winifred Hind died, George and his Swiss wife Ruth took the courageous decision to host Broomhill and sell their own house in Belfast. Eric was also living there and later he told me that their relationship was 'a steep learning curve' for him, as he and George were brought up in such different backgrounds and traditions. However, as time went by, they forged as close a friendship as two intelligent men could have expected! While at Broomhill, George wrote some of his best articles and was asked to contribute to the New Ireland Forum in Dublin in 1983. Sadly, George's health deteriorated and he had to have medical treatment at a nursing home and died in 1997.

The following is an appreciation of a pamphlet on George's life, written in 1999:

'This pamphlet appears at the moment when negotiations on the future of Northern Ireland have reached a point where there are real grounds for hope. Written as a posthumous biography by Dr Roddy Evans, a Southern Irish Anglican and close friend of George, there is an introduction by Father Gerry Reynolds, a Catholic Redemptorist priest, which highlights the collaborative approach to the pamphlet. This would have pleased Dallas as his deep love for his own community led him to dedicate 20 years to learning to understand, and thus improve, the relationships between all communities on the island.

The latter half of the pamphlet is made up of George Dallas' view of reconciliation, which is not sentimental and is a challenge to those who see themselves as British in the Northern Irish community, but Dallas is a visionary and a prophet is seldom accepted in his own country. The pamphlet eloquently expresses the effect of the past 200 years on the mind-set of Protestants and Catholics on both sides of the border. Dallas believed that the situation in Northern Ireland needs the creative cooperation, understanding and repentance of the English who had planted Protestant settlers there and perpetuated the unjust oppression of Catholics and those Protestants used to maintain the system. Dallas believed that the power of ideology fused with the Holy Spirit could be the driving force of radical change in human motivation. This for him meant an acceptance by all peoples of Northern Ireland of their place in an Irish nation which would embrace all the different communities. This was incredibly difficult, as years of polarisation brought a fear of Catholicism, which was seen as intrinsically linked with Irish national identity.

The key, George felt, lay with the Northern Presbyterians. Punished for uniting with the Catholics in an attempt for independence in 1798, they adopted a British identity and from then on looked to Britain for the security of their religion and culture. The intransigence in the Protestants is partly due to the insecurity and alienation of a people who have felt neither accepted as Irish nor British, and at the same time nurtured the feeling of being a special people favoured by God, and unwilling to give up their political supremacy. George felt that dialogue would be inadequate if it was only between political moderates, and through his writings and the remarkable friendships he developed with others of different traditions, he managed in his quiet but honest way to open people's hearts to those whom they had perceived until then as 'them' ".

As John Austin Baker, Anglican Bishop of Salisbury, wrote to George's wife, Ruth, on his death in 1997: "He helped us all to see our own situation in a new light and challenged us to find the courage to acknowledge our common humanity".

Chapter 6

English Trade Unionists

IN THE EARLY 1970s, Eric decided to invite some of his trade union friends in England to come to Belfast. He arranged an evening meeting in the Queen's Hall in down-town Belfast to which men from different factories across Belfast were invited to hear two English trade unionists tell their stories. One of these was a militant docker's leader from the Port of Avonmouth and the other was a building worker from Coventry, who had been a communist and had survived as a Japanese prisoner of war in the construction of the Burma railway; he spoke of how he had lost his hatred of the Japanese and Japan.

Tommy Elwood who was standing at the back of the meeting, was much moved by this story. Tommy was deputy convenor of his trade union in the large engineering firm in Belfast, where in the disturbances in the 1920s, all Catholic workers were driven out of the factory, as they were from other factories. These factories from then on had a reputation of employing only Protestants. That night, listening to the experiences of the man from Coventry, Tommy, an Orangeman, lost his hatred of Catholics.

Tommy then formed some unlikely friendships, one of which was a City councillor, Jack Lavelle, a Catholic from West Belfast who was a member of the Republican Labour Party. Tommy also sorted his relationship with the convenor of his own trade union, Jimmy McIlwaine. Others became interested, including Billy Childs, an Orangeman and a member of the Royal Black Preceptory, and Billy Arnold, Secretary of the Boilermakers' Society. These men and their wives formed a cross community group made up of trade union members.

George Dallas' short pithy play

George Dallas had a gift of recalling the idiomatic conversations of Belfast people, so he wrote a short play illustrating how sectarian attitudes could change, even in the most die-hard people. He was helped with the scripting by Gerry O'Neill, a Catholic trade unionist from West Belfast. George then invited Tommy, Jimmy, and their wives and others to take parts in play readings to invited audiences, while meantime bombs exploded and conflict raged in the streets of Belfast. The group then went to different parts of Ireland, including Wexford and Derry, paid a visit to the Irish Parliament and met with the Irish President in Dublin in the early 1980s.

This experiment in healing sectarian hatred caught the attention of a Canadian, Dr Paul Campbell, then living with his family in London. He was concerned about the situation in Canada at that time, when nationalism had turned to violence and the Quebec Minister of Labour, Pierre Laporte, was taken hostage and later found dead in the trunk of a car. Paul Campbell came to Belfast to meet the trade union men and he suggested to them that they might advance their own situation in Northern Ireland if they helped with the situation in Canada. "Why not come to Canada with your play?" he asked. So began the first of what turned out to be several visits across the Atlantic to Canada, where they travelled to Montreal, Trois-Rivières, Quebec City, Ottawa and the far west, Alberta and British Columbia.

The group then went to the U.S.A. where Eric felt very much at home again. At a meeting in the State Department in Washington, attended by the heads of the Irish, British and other European desks, the officials were keen to meet people from the 'grass roots' in Northern Ireland – folk they regarded as the 'nuts and bolts' of the problem! Jack Lavelle then took the opportunity to vent Catholic anger at the events of 'Bloody Sunday' in the City of Derry, when paratroopers had opened fire on an unarmed civil rights march, killing 14 people and wounding many others. His Protestant colleagues became more and more incensed as Jack hogged the occasion. Billy Childs, especially, was furious and had decided there and then to take the next flight home. After the meeting, the party went for what was only a short walk from the State Department to the Lincoln Memorial. As Billy read Lincoln's Second Inaugural speech engraved on the walls of the Memorial: 'With malice toward none; with charity for all; with firmness in the right, as God gives us to see the right . . .' he found his anger and hatred of Jack Lavelle had melted away.

Laurent Gagnon and Father McCarthy

The visits to North America were responsible for an unexpected turn of events in Northern Ireland. In the mid-1970s, a young French Canadian from Quebec, Laurent Gagnon, arrived in Belfast, to see for himself what was going on. Friends in Belfast made arrangements for him to stay in the home of Billy Arnold and his wife Ivy. Billy was a boilermaker who had worked for many years in the Harland & Wolff shipyard, of *Titanic* fame. As well as being secretary of his union, he later became Chairman of the Boilermakers' Society for Great Britain and Northern Ireland.

At the time Laurent came to his home as a guest, Billy was off work from the yard, as a steel plate had fallen and injured his foot. Billy was a member of the Orange Order, so had little contact with the Catholic nationalist community. How then was Billy to entertain a young French Catholic, he asked himself? He hit on the notion that the best thing would be to take Laurent to visit local Catholic priests. On the third such visit, Billy and Laurent called on the Redemptorists Clonard Monastery and there they met an unusual priest, Father Christopher McCarthy C.Ss.R. Father McCarthy had recently returned from a theological teaching post in Villa Nova University, Philadelphia, U.S.A. Before that he had served in India, Sri Lanka and Australia and previously had been a much-loved Director of a large confraternity at Clonard Monastery. A fellow priest once described Father McCarthy thus: "Some priests are pastors and some priests are explorers but Father Christy is the arch-explorer!" Father McCarthy loved people with an abiding interest in everything about them, who they were and what they did. He was orthodox in his faith and at heart an Irish patriot. Over the next few years, Father McCarthy and Eric formed a close friendship and understanding, for which Father McCarthy would have described with his favourite heartfelt 'Thanks be to God'.

Mrs Ellie McDermott's apology

The young French Canadian visitor then arranged for Father McCarthy to visit the home of Dr Winifred Hind, who was entertaining friends in her home one evening. Father McCarthy went along for the occasion but admitted later that he had not been overly impressed with the people he met, so decided that one visit to the house would be enough. That was until an old lady spoke to him. This was Mrs Ellie McDermott, a widow whose late husband Ernie had been a bank official, and Ellie's father, Sir Frederick Simmons, was war time Mayor of Derry City, and of course, a staunch unionist. This city represented the most notorious case in the Province of unfair elections for the City Council, when the practice of gerrymandering election districts was endemic. The majority of the population in Derry City were Catholic, yet the minority Protestant unionist community contrived to permanently control the City Council.

That evening, which Eric hosted, Ellie McDermott, in the course of a prayer, apologised to Father McCarthy for the way she and her family had behaved in Derry towards his people. Later Father McCarthy said, "The sincerity of the apology from that old lady struck me like a blow in the chest. It was the first time I had heard someone from her class admit to the wrongs that had been done by her people."

Father McCarthy then had a short spell in a Redemptorist Monastery in Limerick, pondering his experience in Belfast. He came to the conclusion that he had a sense of vocation to return to Belfast to attempt to 'remove the myths and misunderstandings from the minds of some of those in the community there'. However, while Father McCarthy knew this was right, he was reluctant to take on such a difficult and daunting task. Then he remembered his reaction to the apology from Mrs McDermott from Derry and with the support of the Rector of the Limerick Monastery, Father McCarthy set off in his car for Belfast. There, with the help of Jim Lynn, the story of the Clonard Bible Study meetings unfolds.

The creation of the Clonard Bible Study, by Jim Lynn

'In the mid 1970s, my brother Paddy Lynn and I, after attending the Monday night Men's Confraternity, went down to a prayer meeting in Clonard Hall. Father Christy McCarthy, a Clonard Redemptorist priest, was also there; he was the director of the Men's Confraternity. At the tea break Father Christy asked the question loudly: "How are we going to bring Protestants and Catholics together? Everything we have tried so far has failed!"

Paddy replied, "Start a Bible study, Father."

"Right, Paddy, and this includes you, Jim – we'll have our first meeting on Thursday evening".

We three met at Clonard Monastery in one of the rooms and it was there that the 'Thursday evening Clonard Bible Study' was founded.

Each Thursday at 7.30 pm we would gather together to share the word of God. The Bible study was gathering new members as the weeks went by and from a personal point of view, I was delighted, as they were all Catholics. Then one Thursday evening Father Christy asked me to stay back; he told me he had met a group of Protestant men and women who were quite extraordinary and felt that I should meet them. I told him I really was not keen on this as I had had some bad experiences with Protestants; nevertheless I was willing to give it a go. Father Christy told me that they would be attending the following Thursday – and his second piece of 'good news' was that he himself was not able to be there!

The following Thursday, the Bible study group were waiting expectantly on the arrival of Father Christy's friends. At 7.30 pm there was a light knock on the door and one of us went over to open it. As I looked on with interest, into the room walked Bill and Muriel Porter, with Eric Turpin, members of the Anglican Communion. We greeted each other and then settled down to read the scriptures for that evening; the Bible study was a flowing study of scripture with everyone having a say.

On another Thursday evening, as we were reading the scripture, there arose the sentence 'Jesus and his brothers and sisters'. Eric mentioned this and as chairman I realised that this was a very important moment. So I said,

"We as Roman Catholics, Eric, do not believe that Jesus had brothers or sisters of the flesh, as we are all his brothers and sisters".

I had a sense that the future of the Bible study hung on Eric's answer. And at that moment, we witnessed the Holy Spirit working through Eric. He replied,

"Let us leave this to the theologians, Jim; we have more that unites us here than that which divides us."

I often spoke of this to Eric, as we both knew that his answer was Spirit-led for the Bible group so that we might realise 'what is God's plan for both Ireland and England for the world.'

Another event which I remember well was when we were speaking of what the evening readings meant to each other, I asked the question,

"Who loves England the most?"

Some shrugged their shoulders and Eric wasn't sure and said,

"Who do you say loves England the most, Jim?"

I replied,

"Those who love England the most are the Blue Bloods, the Church, and the Army."

Eric nearly fell out of his chair when he heard this and kept repeating, "Say that again; say that again". He was deeply moved, as were the others in the group.

Another miraculous moment was when Leslie Fox, an Englishman over from All Saints Anglican church in Dulwich, London, was visiting us one Thursday. Leslie later wrote an article in *The Irish Times* describing what happened to him that evening:

"I resisted for some time that my country's past policies were in any way responsible for the troubles in Northern Ireland. Then when I was present at a Bible Group at Clonard, I read in Chapter 3 of 2nd Peter: 'He does not wish any to perish, but all to betake them to repentance.' I had been studying the history of Ireland, and those words riveted for me the thought that I and my country need to repent and change."

Looking back, there is no doubt that these were quite extraordinary people; their presence and contribution enriched the whole of those evening Bible studies. I can say that keen as I was on a Catholic Bible study, God had other plans for the group and allowed us to see the Thursday evening Bible study prosper and grow in numbers and people began to come from all parts of Belfast: the Shankill Road, the Falls, Mission halls and Christians from Holywood and East Belfast, and also quite a lot from England, including the late Bishop John Austin Baker and Canon Desmond Parsons, leaders of the Anglican Church.

As chairperson of the Bible study, I now know that the presence of Eric Turpin and Bill and Muriel Porter, who were associated with Moral Re-Armament, brought the Bible study to a new level. In saying 'Yes' to them to come to Clonard allowed the Holy Spirit to bring us closer together in our journey for His plan for each of us and our countries. The standards which they lived by were the four absolutes, Love, Purity, Honesty and Unselfishness – which somehow did manage to rub off onto the rest of us!'

Jim Lynn
Belfast

'Belfast Report'

After the initiatives with George's play readings across Ireland and the visits to North America, a decision was made to make a short film telling the story of the developing understanding and change of attitude that had developed between some individuals from the Catholic and Protestant communities in Northern Ireland.

Eric knew a BBC film-maker, Hannen Foss, and his colleague, Peter Sisam, and they agreed to undertake the venture. The resulting documentary film they made was called 'Belfast Report'. These were the actual stories told by the different individuals, in their own words: colourful and not without humour!

One Saturday morning in Clonard Monastery, Father McCarthy arranged a showing of the film for Gerry Adams and his uncle Liam Hannaway. At the close of the screening, Adams commented, "This is one of the best presentations of its kind that I have seen. However, it misses the point. The fundamental issue here is the relationship between the two nations, Ireland and England. Sectarian division in the Province is a secondary issue."

Nobody present at the occasion could fault that observation.

Chapter 7

England and the English

PROVIDENTIALLY, THERE WAS an entry to England through Dulwich, in London. The Rev Desmond Parsons, the Rector of All Saints Church, had a weekly discussion group for men in his parish, and at one of those meetings, someone asked, "We have discussed many topics at these meetings but so far we have said nothing about what is happening in the apparently never-ending civil strife in a part of our own country. Does anyone in this group have contacts in Northern Ireland and would they invite some people from there to come and speak to us?" Leslie Fox, who was a member of the discussion group, told them he had friends in Belfast and would make enquiries to see if some of them might come over to meet the group.

The request from All Saint's Church was promptly answered by Father McCarthy. He brought a group of Protestant loyalists and Catholic nationalists to Dulwich, who were made welcome in the homes of the parishioners of All Saints. A meeting was arranged in Tom and Ida Garrud's home; Tom was a lay reader in the church and a director of the *Daily Mail*. So from this beginning an ongoing link grew between All Saints Church and Clonard Monastery, with several more visits and exchanges.

John Austin Baker

The Rev John Austin Baker was Rector of St. Margaret's Church, Westminster and Anglican Chaplain to the Speaker of the House of Commons. In response to Pope John Paul's visit to Ireland in 1979, Canon Baker felt he should make a statement from his pulpit, in which he expressed his sense of shame at what his country England had done to Ireland over the centuries. Unusually, he decided to issue his sermon to the press, and the Irish newspapers carried it widely. As a result of hearing about this, Father McCarthy decided on another visit to London to call on Canon Baker. So a strong link was established between the Church of England and Churches in Belfast and elsewhere in the Province. This confirmed a conviction expressed by a member of Father McCarthy's Bible study group at Clonard Monastery:

"The true heart of England resides in the Church of England, the aristocracy and the army. That heart is still sound and with a renewed heart, could halt the decline of a great nation."

In January every year Christians throughout the world set aside a week for prayers for Christian unity. At one of these weeks, Father McCarthy arranged services in Clonard Church and invited Canon Baker to preach there. Later, when John Austin Baker was appointed as Bishop of Salisbury, he had the distinction and privilege of being the first Anglican Bishop to preach at St. Patrick's Cathedral, Armagh, at the invitation of the Catholic Primate, Cardinal Tomas O Fiaich. Bishop Baker also met with political and church leaders from both communities during the course of a number of visits, when he and his wife Jill were guests of George and Ruth Dallas, along with Eric.

Joan Tapsfield

Another unexpected but welcome arrival on the scene from England was Miss Joan Tapsfield who was a retired English senior civil servant living in Kent. One evening watching the news from Northern Ireland on the TV, she found herself wondering how her fellow civil servants were coping with working in Northern Ireland. She felt she ought to find out, so she wrote to a friend, Miss Kitty Montgomery, and asked her if she could come and visit her.

Kitty was glad to welcome Joan to her home in Derry. However, this turned out to have a more dramatic outcome than either of them expected, as Joan wrote about it later, describing her second visit to Derry which coincided with their Civic Week. This included an exhibition in the University called 'Emigration'; Joan wrote that she had been studying a bit of the history of Derry and the neighbouring ports of Inishowen, which had seen many farewells of the people who left Ireland in their thousands in the mid-nineteenth century. Some of the shipping companies provided a few loaves for the four to five weeks journey, but many passengers, already exhausted by famine, died *en route* and the ships became known as 'coffin ships'.

The way this history was told seemed to confirm an impression Joan had that England, at that time responsible for the whole of Ireland, was being blamed for all these tragedies, and this was an idea she strenuously resisted, attributing it to 'left-wing propaganda'. But she was troubled about it.

Driving around Inishowen with her friend Kitty on a lovely summer day, they visited a little Catholic church where there were vivid pictures of the Stations of the Cross, and the one that caught her eye was where Pilate was washing his hands to disclaim responsibility for the death of Jesus. She wrote:

"It struck me then, like lightning, that Pilate was a typical official, not deliberately wicked but sacrificing truth to expediency, and perhaps, typical of officialdom in our own time, and certainly of my resistance to accepting the truth of the damage my country had done to Ireland. Kneeling down, I prayed for forgiveness for myself and my country and for the courage to do whatever God wanted."

After a few more visits and consulting her Irish friends, she decided to sell her house in Kent and move to Northern Ireland, "as a drop in the ocean of the restitution we owed to the Irish, of whom so many had been forced to leave their homes. I have grown to love Ireland, but the mainspring of my move was a love of my country England. If my father, for whom I had great affection and respect, had died in debt, I should have wanted to repay the debt. I feel the same about my country. To face the past is not to forego our patriotism but to enhance it."

From 'An English Pilgrim in Northern Ireland 1977-1992' – Joan Tapsfield

A visit to Australia – and back

Joan spent eighteen years in Northern Ireland, initially in Derry where she bought a house and likewise later in Belfast. One memorable visit, among many, was a visit to Australia, when a group had been invited to take part in an MRA conference in Perth in 1979. Joan was accompanied by three others: Father McCarthy, who knew the country well from earlier years there as a Redemptorist priest; Billy Childs, a crane driver from the Port of Belfast and an Orangeman, and Eric.

While attending the conference, they were interviewed on a popular Sunday television programme, as the producers were eager to have the views

From left to right: Father McCarthy, Billy Childs, Eric Turpin, Joan Tapsfield

of such a diverse group on what was happening in Northern Ireland. The anchor-man of the programme was a Reverend and he couldn't get over how all the participants had their say, without shouting at or abusing each other, despite such apparently contrary opinions. It was a lively occasion, making excellent television.

From Perth, they went to Adelaide, Melbourne and Canberra, meeting a wide cross-section of people. In Canberra they met with a Catholic Bishop and during this meeting Eric corrected Father McCarthy because he felt Father McCarthy had been 'too hard' on Billy Childs, the Orangeman. The following morning Eric suddenly contracted a severe middle-ear infection, probably from swimming in the pool where he was staying. This left him feeling very dizzy and sick and prevented him from travelling with the group to Brisbane, Sydney and Toowoomba. He didn't catch up with the others until a week later, as they were all leaving from Sydney to fly home to Belfast.

While waiting for a connecting flight at Schipol airport, Eric apologised to Father McCarthy for 'putting him down' in front of his own Bishop, during the meeting in Canberra. Father McCarthy's response was that he had intended to raise it with Eric the next day and insist on an apology, which if he had not received from Eric, he would have flown straight back to Belfast; indeed, he had already enquired about an available flight. However, the culprit had not turned up, so Father McCarthy felt he should put it aside until Eric had recovered his health.

Later, Father McCarthy commented that 'MRA must be very important to God for Him to have done that to Eric'. Strangely, the experience brought the two men closer together and developed a complete trust between them.

Challenge facing Britain on Northern Ireland

From an article in *The Irish Times* on 18th November 1981 by **Leslie Fox** of All Saints Church, Dulwich, England:

'British policies and actions in the past have led to the present intractable situation in Northern Ireland, the Moral Re-Armament movement was told recently.

In an address given at the movement's headquarters in Caux, Switzerland, its Treasurer, Mr Leslie Fox, a London accountant said:

"We British are worried about our inability to see any end to the troubles in Northern Ireland. This may be an inducement for us to consider the underlying causes of this problem, which is perhaps the most intractable in the world today.

For us British the tendency is to think that our job is to go into Northern Ireland to help these feuding Irishmen to sort it out. But there is another element in the deadlock and that is Britain. It is British policies and actions in the past that have led to the present intractable situation.

There is a seamy side to the English character, along with our ignorance of Irish history: a ruthlessness, deceit, divisiveness, superiority, indifference to suffering and the toleration of injustice. The question one faces, has our character changed? Or are some of these same elements I have described still in our character and at work today?

But an altogether more positive question we can and should ask ourselves: is God wanting to use the anvil of the Irish problem to hammer out our character into a new shape for His purposes?

Some British people feel a sense of guilt about Ireland. But there is a difference between guilt and repentance. Guilt means you shun the people you feel guilty about. Repentance means that you turn to God for forgiveness. He opens you heart to those you have wronged, even if you cannot put everything right...

History plays an important part in today's situation. Reading about it recently, I discovered that since 1848 when the Catholic population in Ulster rose to over 40%, the Protestants feared they would be overwhelmed. This led to the exclusion of Catholics from Protestant areas of housing and employment. In recent years discrimination over housing has been eliminated and the Government is doing its best to eliminate discrimination over jobs. But in spite of new policies, what happens at street level is rather different. In some Catholic areas over 50% are out of work and there is a feeling of hopelessness. A Catholic friend of mine said, "While you have injustice you will have the IRA..."

And what about the wrongs we have done to the Protestant community? Canon Baker, the Chaplain to the House of Commons, was quoted in a Dublin paper *The Irish Independent,* saying: "We, the British, are also largely responsible for the fears and problems felt by the Protestant community in Northern Ireland. Having put them there to maintain an all-Ireland Union with Great Britain and encouraged them for generations to build their lives around this, then we suddenly turned about and tried to abandon them to the very situation they had been taught to resist at all costs."

If we British are ever to find some light at the end of the long dark tunnel of Northern Ireland, we have to face the past and what it reveals about our character, examine our personal and national behaviour today, recognising that our character is just the same as it was in the past. If we do this, we can seek forgiveness from God and then face the present with new honesty.

To change the character of a nation takes time. Wilberforce did it for England in the 18th century when the abolition of the slave trade was the issue. It took a lifetime but it worked.

This is the challenge, focused by Northern Ireland, which is facing us as a nation today: to be honest with ourselves, to see what constructive changes are demanded of the British people and then to meet and study and pray and

A delegation from Northern Ireland meets the Secretary of State for Northern Ireland at the Westminster Parliament to share their experiences of MRA's peace and reconciliation activities in the Province

work until those changes take place. We shall need the help of others and other nations in this task.

Father McCarthy of Clonard Monastery has what he calls a 'dazzling vision' of what England and Ireland working together could do for the rest of the world. What hope and fresh direction these two nations, united, could give to every hopeless situation in the world!

That is what God is calling some of us to. And I for one am ready to answer that call."

Chapter 8

The Anglo-Irish

IN FEBRUARY 1977 the Church of Ireland's 'Role of the Church Committee' issued a document calling for 'penitence, honesty, realism and determination to face radical change' and that there was still time 'for Churches, Governments and others to make a positive contribution to the creation of a society for which we all long.' Seeing this as an opportunity to express their views on the situation, Eric, Roddy Evans, and Bill and Muriel Porter decided to issue a joint press statement expressing some of the unacknowledged history of their Ascendancy Church. However, before issuing it, they felt they ought to check it with their Archbishop Dr George Otto Simms. When they visited the Archbishop's home with their document, he read it swiftly and then handed it to his wife, Mercy, for her considered opinion. As an historian and a scholar, she read it through carefully, and then said forcefully,

"This should have been issued years ago and it should have been done officially by the Church." Then she asked rhetorically,

"Why is it necessary? Because our attitudes are just the same and given the opportunity, we would do the same things all over again."

She advised that it should be issued publicly on the opening day of what she referred to as 'that pagan jamboree', the Church of Ireland General Synod, which was about to take place in May in Dublin.

In that month there was an MRA conference taking place in London on the subject of the British Commonwealth, and the statement was read to the conference delegates by one of the signatories. As soon as it was issued, BBC Radio Ulster was on the phone to the conference venue from Belfast, seeking a live interview, and the daily newspapers in Ireland carried reports next day, including *The Irish Times*, which placed it in the centre of their page reporting the opening day of the General Synod. Here is part of their statement:

'Prior to 1800, the Protestant Ascendancy that ruled the Dublin Parliament was the Ascendancy of the Church of Ireland. So the Penal Laws were to some extent also applied to Presbyterians. They, like Catholics, could not hold office under the Crown. They, like Catholics, were forced to pay tithes to help finance the Church of Ireland.

For these and other reasons Presbyterians migrated in tens of thousands to the United States. In the War of Independence they, through their sense of grievance, helped form the backbone of Washington's army.

But what we, as members of the Ascendancy Church, did to the Catholics, was infamous beyond belief. As the Chief Justice of the day said, 'The law does not suppose any such person to exist as an Irish Roman Catholic.' By our studied and deliberate degradation of a proud and cultured people, we reduced them to a poverty stricken peasantry bereft of their natural leaders. We hounded their priests and denied them all possibility of education.

We therefore set in train events that led eventually and inevitably to the starvation of the famine years from 1845 onwards. This meant migration by the hundred thousand to the United States.

We are deeply sorry for these and many other such deeds, not in the spirit of breast-beating, but in honesty and penitence. We know that we must realistically face them if we are ever to be trusted in the future.

We know of many other situations in the world where an honest and penitent facing of the facts, instead of excusing ourselves, could lead to 'the creation of a society for which we all long.' It is to this end that we sign this document.

Each of us has lived in the North of Ireland for a number of years; was born in the South of Ireland; is a confirmed member of the Church of Ireland; is a graduate of Trinity College Dublin; believes we cannot expect our leaders to do and say what we are not prepared to do and say ourselves.'

James Roderick Evans, F.R.C.S.I.	Elizabeth Muriel Porter, B.A.
Samuel Eric Turpin, M.Sc.	William Arthur Porter, B.A.

The publication of the document meant a lot to both George Dallas and Alec McRitchie, who are both Presbyterians in Northern Ireland, as it gave them a sense of closure on the past and encouragement for the future of their country.

Two Protestant Cathedrals in Dublin

Another rather extraordinary aspect of Anglo-Irish life is that the Anglican Church of Ireland still owns both ancient Cathedrals in Dublin, St. Patrick's and Christ Church, while the Irish Catholic Church has had to 'make do' with a Pro Cathedral in a side street. This dates back to 1691 when the English King offered Irish Catholics the freedom of their religion, half the churches in Ireland and a share of their ancient possessions. But the Dublin parliament, which was entirely Anglo-Irish, reversed the King's promise. So all the old churches across Ireland have remained the property of the Protestant Ascendancy ever since then.

When Pope John Paul II made his historic visit to Ireland in 1979, Eric and friends saw this as an opportunity for a generous gesture by the Church of Ireland to return at least one of the Cathedrals to their fellow Catholic countrymen. They discussed this with Father McCarthy, who felt that the older of the two, Christ Church, would be the most significant. So they got in touch with the Chairman of the Representative Church Body, John Biggs, who undertook to raise this with the Standing Committee. However, when John Biggs came back with the reply, he had to tell the intrepid group that the answer was "No" adding that the Committee were 'vehemently' opposed to such a suggestion.

Undeterred, but with no great anticipation it would produce a result, one of the group wrote a letter that was published by the Church of Ireland weekly *Gazette* thus: 'The return of Christ Church Cathedral, apart from being an act of Christian restitution, would have the additional non spiritual merit of considerable financial saving. The upkeep of two Cathedrals so near to each other in the same city is a heavy burden to bear.' Bear it they did – and still do.

The stories in Chapter 7 and Chapter 8 are taken from 'Where I sensed *The Breath of God*: A Footnote in Anglo-Irish History' by Dr Roddy Evans.

Chapter 9

A chance encounter

ERIC WROTE THIS story personally and it is an account of a difficult experience that moved him deeply, for the reason he describes in the penultimate paragraph.

"This is the story of my last visit to Caux which I attended for ten days, along with some English delegates. The usual conference procedure was that a main meeting was held in the mornings, where people from a number of different countries told of their experiences. In the afternoon, there would be a series of smaller meetings, usually of different national groups. As the morning meetings were held in a variety of different languages, translation was provided, while in the afternoons, there was only one language – something of a blessing for an old chap like me! So, one afternoon I decided to go to the English meeting, where I found I was the only Irish person there.

Part of the focus of that particular gathering was to prepare for the following day's main meeting, at which Cardinal Koenig would be the principal guest. The question was posed: what story or experience did the English present at Caux have that might be of interest to the Cardinal? Now, I had worked for several years in England and I knew how stilted and formal such meetings could sometimes be, whereas since those years in England, I had been in Belfast, where meetings were more informal and even disorganised! I was hoping, that afternoon at Caux, that someone might say, 'Have you anything to contribute from Ireland, Eric?' But nobody asked me.

When the meeting ended, I went for a walk up the hill with a Scottish friend and suddenly I began to weep uncontrollably. This was something I had never experienced before or since. I could neither explain it nor understand it.

It was just a great sense of hopelessness and isolation from God and man. I returned to my room, washed my face and tried to look respectable, as I was to have a meal with two men from Zimbabwe and another friend from Scotland who had lived in that country. As I was walking towards the table, a lady who had been at the afternoon meeting and was part French, stopped me and said, "Eric, we never asked you what you thought." With that I burst into tears again and had to hurry back to my room once more, to tidy up.

Eventually, I returned to the dining room and joined the table with the two Zimbabweans and the Scot, and to my amazement, another person was sitting at the table, Cardinal Koenig. He had just arrived at Caux and as was the custom on such occasions, a special table had been arranged for him to meet various interesting people. However, he had come to the dining room rather earlier than expected and had chosen to sit at the table where he saw two Africans.

I was able to tell the Cardinal our experiences in Ireland and what I was learning about Presbyterians and Catholics and of our visits to America. Then I told him of my experience of weeping that afternoon. He seemed interested in all this and later I heard he had commented he was glad to see the Holy Spirit had not left the house. Some days later, as the Cardinal was leaving the conference, I asked him how on earth he had chosen to sit at that particular table, on that first night. In reply, he pointed to the sky.

It was, however, all of six months before the reason for my weeping came clear to me: I felt that England would never understand the position in Ireland or acknowledge the part she had played in it all.

Since that event in Caux, I corresponded with Cardinal Koenig and he wrote that he hoped to come someday to Ireland. However, sadly, he died in Vienna, aged 98."

The death of a dear friend, Father McCarthy

Another moving experience for Eric was the death of his dear friend and colleague, Father Christopher McCarthy, in 1983. I well remember Eric being in tears at the funeral in the Clonard Church; he said to me that he felt 'our work is over without Father McCarthy', but happily and providentially, this was not so, as others battled on together.

Father Alec Reid, a fellow Redemptorist, wrote in this tribute to Father McCarthy in the Belfast morning paper *The Irish News* on the 16th August 1983:

'Father Christy will be remembered with esteem and affection by the many people, Protestant and Catholic, whom he inspired when they came to know and work with him in Belfast. He directed a magnificent apostolate for Christian reconciliation and peace. This was to be the last, and many would say, the most glorious chapter in the story of his missionary enterprises because now he was braving the pain and difficulties of a crippling illness andat the same time, breaking new paths across the dangerous lines of prejudice and misunderstanding that so divide the people of Northern Ireland.

Showing all the old drive and initiative and with a dauntless trust in God that enabled him to rise to heroic heights of courage and determination, he helped to organise new points of contact between Catholics and Protestants so that, by praying and studying regularly together, they might share their hopes and plans for peace. The members of Moral Re-Armament were closely associated with him in this apostolate and their friendship was a tower of strength and comfort during his final years. Together they contacted people in England who were deeply concerned about the situation in Ireland. Among them was John Austin Baker, Bishop of Salisbury. A man of great vision and integrity and with a deep love for the people of Ireland, he became, at Father McCarthy's request, the first Protestant pastor to preach in a Catholic church in Belfast.'

'Where I sensed the Breath of God'

As Roddy Evans writes in the last paragraph of his booklet, 'Where I Sensed the Breath of God', "With the gift of hindsight, like a golden thread, the events that are recorded here, humanly unplanned, have followed one another in a remarkably ordered sequence. Father McCarthy would have unquestionably attributed this to the leading of the Holy Spirit".

Cradle of the Peace Process

Then finally, Eric could see and experience the joy and gladness of all those who had 'laboured in the vineyard' for decades, when the Good Friday

Agreement brought peace. Anne Cadwallader, a feature writer for *Ireland on Sunday* wrote an article on the 12th December 1999, printed here in part:

On a place which played a vital role in the North's long and winding road to democracy

'Although the public pageantry of the peace process has taken place against the splendour of Stormont, its birthplace and cradle was Clonard Monastery in West Belfast, now celebrating a century's working in the midst of the troubles. Clonard, whose high altar is just one hundred yards from the Falls/Shankill peace line and whose walls bear silent witness to the pogroms of the 1920s and the burning of Bombay Street in 1969, has more than earned its place in the hearts of people across Ireland.

The Monastery, dedicated to the Most Holy Redeemer, was built in just three years, paid for from the public subscriptions of the poverty-stricken mill workers who lived around it in the early years of the century. So it was perhaps fitting that its walls witnessed the first meetings between Gerry Adams and John Hume, brought together by Father Alex Reid, one of the Redemptorist priests of the Monastery, to talk about building peace, as long ago as 1988.

In the words of John Austin Baker, Anglican Bishop of Salisbury, written in 1983: 'How wonderfully God draws us here to the Falls Road to learn more of what it means to be a Christian and to pledge ourselves, Catholic, Presbyterian, Methodist, Lutheran, Anglican, to live our Christianity together.'

Chapter 10

Some light relief!

AT THE TIME 10 Broomhill Park was being sold, Eric was visiting his doctor and when she discovered he was about to be 'homeless' and had been looking for the right place to live, she immediately told him she knew of a room that was vacant in an Abbeyfield Home. The upshot was that Eric moved into Voysey House in Cadogan Place, where he remained for the rest of his days. He had a ground floor room, with a bow window looking out onto a small front garden, with a garden and lawn at the rear; there were up to six other residents, each with their own room, a communal sitting room and dining room/kitchen. This was a new experience for Eric, who had been used to communal living but generally with those whom he chose to live with! Now there were 'strangers' who swiftly became friends as time went by.

There could be no remembrance of Eric without his three other abiding passions: his skill as a master carpenter, his love and devotion to Westerns, and golf, not necessarily in that order! To begin with the most relaxing, the Westerns; these he read avidly, with a plentiful supply from the local library quite close by. Then in his later years a faithful friend brought them regularly in a bag from

Eric in his wood work shed, Voysey House

Eric with Roddy Evans and David Hume on a golfing outing

the library and returned them when she collected the next batch. How she managed not to bring Eric those he had already read remains her secret!

As to carpentry, nobody knows where his skill sprang from but the results spoke for themselves especially with repairs to smaller furniture such as tables and chairs. However, golf was Eric's main relaxation; his champion was the American Ben Hogan, the top professional golfer in the 1950s, when Eric was in his thirties. Gary Player, the South African golfing hero, remarked that 'the harder I practice, the luckier I get' which was not exactly Eric's practice regime but not far off it! He loved just going out somewhere near where he was living and finding a piece of grass field where he could practice his chipping.

His diaries also mention Duffy, a neighbour's little white fluffy mutt! They made great friends and the dog obviously appeared whenever Eric passed by, and I feel sure the owner was only too delighted to have his dog exercised!

Our usual group of three golfers was Eric, Roddy Evans and me, with a fourth whoever was available. I think the furthest we travelled by car was to Royal Dornock, on the north east sea coast of Scotland, a lovely natural course, which we visited more than once. Perhaps our favourite was the Great

Northern Hotel in Bundoran, Co. Donegal where we got Golden Oldies rates! The golf course is right around the hotel, so we could manage two rounds a day, when we were younger! Eric had a single room, as he snored throughout the night! There was one memorable week at that hotel when we didn't play much golf, as we were glued to the RTE TV in our room watching the Queen's visit to Dublin, a truly historic event, beautifully captured on television.

On several occasions a fourth person in the party was our Canadian friend, Dr Paul Campbell. On one occasion his wife Annjet came along and at one point she was heard to say, "How can grown men play golf so badly and still enjoy it?"!

I have a few of Eric's diaries, and regularly throughout, he records visits to Helen's Bay to play golf at our delightful nine hole course with a fabulous view of Belfast Lough and the South Antrim hills. Another memorable spot was *Blinkbonny*, my brother Douglas' holiday home near Nethybridge, on Speyside, also with a nine hole course. There is a fabulous view of the Cairngorm Mountains from that house; there is a photo of this on my desk as I write: an abiding memento of happy days!

Douglas visited us in Ireland on several occasions; he was always keen to know about the situation and how things were progressing. Of course, golf was one of those activities where you can cast aside all the cares of the day, in a welcome and needed break.

Eric was particularly thoughtful and generous with his presents. The earliest one we have, now rather tattered, is a travel book with every town and land mark in Ireland, many beautifully illustrated by pen sketches. It is inscribed on the opening blank page: 'Wishing David and Ruth many Happy Days exploring Ireland together! From Eric 2nd October 1971'. Our wedding day. And Eric's last present to us was a wonderful volume, 'World Atlas of Golf – the greatest courses and how they are played'.

Some enduring memories of a dear friend and companion for forty or more years. Adieu.

Chapter 11

Our best friend, from Alec and Gaby McRitchie

Alec: For more than 30 years, Eric was our best friend. He had a great sense of humour and enjoyed banter. He had a love for the Holy Spirit which shone through. He gave great care to us and later our three children. I had been working full time for MRA for a number of years in the 1970s before deciding to go into a job. Eric gave me great fellowship when I went to work with the NI Housing Executive and became involved in the redevelopment of Belfast's housing, meeting with community representatives from paramilitary organisations, as well as the Government and Army, against the backdrop of a war. Those often weekly meetings with Eric continued until his death.

Gaby: I met Eric along with twelve other Irish people when I invited the group to address my moral ethics class at college in Montreal. The intention was to enliven the class with real stories of people and their faith during the Troubles rather than the usual theoretical discussions to date. Some years later when I visited Ireland, Eric remembered the occasion and he and George and Ruth Dallas asked me to stay with them and participate in what they were doing.

Alec: When the Clonard Bible Study began in 1979, Eric asked us to join it and every Thursday night for almost a decade, I drove him, George and Ruth Dallas and Gaby to Clonard Monastery off the Falls Road during the Troubles, often past burning vehicles and the noise of gunshots, Army checkpoints, and intimidating crowds. Eric figured I had the right contacts whom I could call on if we were stopped.

Eric, along with Roddy Evans and Bill and Muriel Porter, were from the Ascendancy community which had ruled Ireland on England's behalf for hundreds of years. In the late seventies they published a statement in the media, accepting responsibility as members of that community for injustices that had been caused to the Catholic community and, in an earlier era, the Presbyterian community as well. Also in this public act of repentance, they recommended that one of the two Anglican Cathedrals in Dublin be offered back to the Catholic Church.

Their willingness to speak out publicly, potentially risking their lives, and to accept change themselves greatly interested George Dallas and me as Presbyterians. Their statement together with the experience of the Bible Study at Clonard, and Eric and Gaby's care for George and Ruth at their home at Broomhill Park, helped George enormously, and he made a significant contribution to the New Ireland Forum. George's radical thinking for the time has been beautifully captured in a series of booklets by Roddy Evans which are published on the University of Ulster website www.cain.ulst.ac.uk.

Eric's encouragement of English friends to attend Clonard and the extension of links with All Saints Church in Dulwich, London, were part of his strong belief that with change, a reconciled England and Ireland together could give something great to the world.

Both: Most of all we will miss the chats – often in earlier years during golf outings; about his travels and friends he made during his time in Australia, New York, and Montreal which he loved; about science which, as a trained chemist, he loved too, and about personal finance. At the age of 60, on one of his frequent walks to the library, Eric had a clear sense that he would need money to finance his old age – a good call, as he lived to 95. His experience of learning about investing and seeking God's help with it was inspiring to anyone with an interest in money. It enabled him not only to finance his last very happy 15 years in a wonderful Abbeyfield Society home but to be generous to many friends, including our family.

Alec and Gaby McRitchie
Belfast, 11 November 2014

In fond remembrance

Eric passed away peacefully in his sleep in the Voysey House Abbeyfield in Belfast on the morning of Monday 20th October 2014. With him as he breathed his last was the Rev. Canon Robert Jones, who had been phoned by the staff when they were unable to waken Eric. Shortly afterwards Kathleen Kennedy, Eric's niece and her husband Desmond, arrived by car from their home in Sligo, and they were together able to arrange the funeral for the following Friday the 24th October. This was a Funeral Service of Thanksgiving in the Church of Saint John the Evangelist, Parish of Malone, Belfast, which had been Eric's church for over 30 years, and where his ashes were later interned.

So passed on the life, at the age of 95, of a truly remarkable Irishman. At the funeral, the Rev. Robert Jones told us that he had only known Eric for the two years since he had been appointed Rector to St. John's but in that time, Eric had been able to come to the mid-week communion and coffee chat afterwards. Turning to Eric's life's work, he described how Eric, when he was attending Trinity College, Dublin, had met up with the Oxford Group Moral Re-Armament.

The Rector gave a picture of how Eric had then travelled across the continents and had taken on to work with the dockers of the world; this had included Brooklyn in New York, USA (which Robert wasn't at all sure he himself would want to visit, after Eric's description of the mafia there!). Also in Canada, Australia and England, and since the 1970s, his beloved Ireland in turmoil, where he wanted to do whatever he could to help.

The Rector added that although Eric had never married, he loved children and would regularly come to the monthly children's service at St. John's, where the children would sit up front together and take part. He also loved his regular visits to Sligo to spend time with his niece, Kathleen Kennedy, great-niece Katherine Regan and great-great nephew and nieces Samuel, Katie and Ciara to whom this book is dedicated. Then the Rector said, "Even in his last months, when he was confined to a chair or bed, Eric never lost either his care for others or his world view".

Two younger women read the lessons, the first being Katherine Regan, Eric's great-niece and the second was our daughter Frances Hume; they discovered later at the funeral that they were almost twins, in that they were born in the same year, month and even week! Frances had asked to say something of what Eric had meant to her, which follows next, to end this story.

Eric with great-great nephew and nieces, Samuel, Katie and Ciara, circa 2012

Frances Hume remembers Eric

I asked if I could say a few words about my memories of Uncle Eric. I actually found out just before boarding a plane in Glasgow last night so forgive me if I have left anything out! Someone said to me, that's nice of you to fly over for the funeral, but how could I not? Uncle Eric meant the world to me.

He was not actually a blood relative, but has been a close member of my family for as long as we can remember. He came to live with my Mum's family when he was in his early 20s and she was seven. At Trinity College he had got involved in a 'spiritual movement for social change' and had a deep conviction to dedicate his life to this, something my grandfather had also done, and this lead Eric on many adventures across the world.

My memories of Uncle Eric began when he was in his early 60s and staying in Belfast with Ruth and George Dallas in a house that belonged to the spiritual movement. It was during the heart of the Troubles and there would be a meeting in the house every Thursday, affectionately called the 'Thursday ladies' as it consisted mainly of women and a small scattering of men, mainly Eric, George, Roddy and my dad. We would all have lunch and then there would be a talk on how we could, to use Mahatma Gandhi's words, 'Be the change you wish to see in the world'.

During the lunch, the women would sit in the living room eating their sandwiches that they had brought with them, while the men, who had the sole advantage of being men, had their lunch made for them by Ruth and sat at the dining room table. At the risk of being terribly gender stereotypical, I discovered at a young age that the ladies' lunchtime chat was rather boring to me, so I would sneak into the men's lunch and listen to them discussing politics, enraptured by their talk of the world, what was going on in it and how we could make a difference in it. For me it was normal to be surrounded by these great men who had dedicated their whole lives and being to God, not just in a 'spiritual' way but in a practical way to do something for others and the world, and to do their bit to bring peace and understanding between nations and promote social justice and human rights.

My best friend said to me that I was lucky to have had such an upbringing, and it has, no doubt about it, set me on my life's course, first working in India, then with Christian Aid and refugees in Glasgow and latterly in interfaith dialogue, bringing people together from different religions and cultures. In fact, it was Uncle Eric who planted the seed in my mind of going to India, although he didn't realise it at the time. I had survived a degree in theology and he told me that I really ought to do something practical with my life now. He challenged me to find my life's calling. His mantra for me when I was feeling a bit lost or low was one that he had been given by the leader of the spiritual movement when Eric himself had felt lost and low, "Get out of yourself and use your heart".

That is something that Eric did with consistency. It is right to remember all the wonderful things that he has done across the world but I imagine, for those of us gathered today, the abiding thing that we will remember is Uncle Eric's big heart for others. Though sometimes hard on himself, he always saw the light in others, and even if it wasn't evident at first, he would do his best to find it. He was one of those rare people who really genuinely cared and took an interest in everybody he came in contact with and I know a number of us have worried about how we are going to cope without his light in our lives today

For the last 15 years Eric stayed in an Abbeyfield home in Belfast, and we are so grateful to the Abbeyfield that he was enabled to stay there as he became less mobile and able to look after himself. I would have been 23 when he moved into the home, just back from India and needing some direction in my life. There is a lovely Gaelic phrase *anam cara* which translates as 'friend of the soul' and in the ancient Celtic Christian tradition, a soul friend would support you with spiritual advice throughout your life journey; Eric was certainly an 'anam cara' in my life.

When I moved to Glasgow in 1999, I looked forward to my visits home and in that 15 years I can only remember two or three occasions when a visit home did not include a visit to Uncle Eric. He would always greet me in his inimitable fashion, with a twinkle in his eye and a cheeky grin! He was always interested in what I was up to, my spiritual ideas and views on world issues, even my love life! I'm sorry he never got to see me walk down the aisle as he had hoped! And he extended this interest and enthusiasm with everybody.

He may have been in a 'retirement home' but his mind and his heart were on fire. Alongside his love for 'cowboy' books, he developed a fascination with quantum physics, and I would marvel that I had just been to have tea with a 90 year old who was grappling enthusiastically with new insights into the nature of reality! While Eric had spent his early years making a difference on the world stage he showed me that your world stage is also here and now with the people who surround you.

He really cared about all the people he shared his life with. I heard stories about Mr Honeyman and the other housemates at the Abbeyfield, about Theresa and the other staff and how much they cared, about Katie and the Bible study group, visits from Daniel McRitchie and of course tales of his wonderful family in Sligo, all of whom are here celebrating his life with us today. He showed me that you didn't have to be physically mobile if you were emotionally mobile. Even in his last weeks as he needed more physical care from carers who would come in several times a day, he didn't appear to complain. He said to me, "This is a new and interesting phase in my life. I'm finding out so much about my new helpers and making new friends, it's like a new chapter". Well, what can I say, the chapter he is on now is very well deserved, and we wish him well, with all the love in the world.